Mediteri

C000154833

Recipes

Vibrant and Healthy Recipes you can Cook Easily

for Eating Well and with Taste Every Day

Amanda Young

with the express written consent from the Publisher. All additional right reserved.

The information in the following pages is broadly considered a truthful and accurate account of facts and as such, any inattention, use, or misuse of the information in question by the reader will render any resulting actions solely under their purview. There are no scenarios in which the publisher or the original author of this work can be in any fashion deemed liable for any hardship or damages that may befall them after undertaking information described herein.

Additionally, the information in the following pages is intended only for informational purposes and should thus be thought of as universal. As befitting its nature, it is presented without assurance regarding its prolonged validity or interim quality. Trademarks that are mentioned are done without written consent and can in no way be considered an endorsement from the trademark holder.

TABLE OF CONTENT

Introduction

The term Mediterranean Diet means a dietary style made of rules and habits inspired by the Mediterranean tradition.

In the fifties of the last century, Ancel Keys, an American nutritionist, noticed that the populations of the Mediterranean basin were less susceptible to some pathologies than the Americans.

From this observation was born the hypothesis that the Mediterranean diet was able to increase the longevity of those who followed it.

The "Seven Countries Study" for twenty years monitored the diet and health conditions of 12,000 people aged between 40 and 60 years, living in different countries such as Japan, the USA, Holland, Yugoslavia, Finland, and Italy.

Keys' initial hypothesis was at that point confirmed and the Mediterranean diet was proposed to the whole world as the ideal food regimen.

Starting from the '70s they tried to spread the typical eating habits of the Mediterranean diet in the United States as well. Cereals, vegetables, fruits, fish, and olive oil were proposed as an alternative to a diet too rich in fats, proteins, and sugars.

The Mediterranean diet is mainly focused on the correct choice of foods, whereas the caloric aspect plays a secondary role. Sobriety and moderation of portions represent however an essential element for the correct application of this diet.

The Mediterranean diet is ideal for preventing and combating many diseases such as arteriosclerosis, heart disease, hypertension, diabetes, tumors, and many others.

The Mediterranean Diet also represents a historical and cultural heritage of great importance and it is proposed as a symbol of a cuisine whose simplicity, fantasy, and flavors are appreciated all over the world.

The typical dishes of the Mediterranean Diet, therefore, represent gastronomic and nutritional excellence of the highest order. The short cooking exalts the perfumes and the flavors of all the ingredients, each of which expresses decisive nutritive and protective properties.

RECIPES

Breakfast Green Smoothie

Prep Time: 7 mins **Cook Time:** 0 mins **Total Time:** 7 mins

MAKES 2 SERVING

INGREDIENTS

- ❖ 2 cups spinach
- ❖ 2 cups kale
- ❖ 1 cup bok choy
- ❖ 1 ½ cup organic almond milk
- ❖ 1 tablespoon almonds, chopped
- ❖ ½ cup of water

INSTRUCTIONS

1. Place all ingredients in the blender and blend until you get a smooth mixture. Pour the smoothie into the serving glasses.
2. Add ice cubes if desired.

Blueberry Banana Protein Smoothie

Prep Time: 5 mins **Cook Time:** 5 mins **Total Time:** 10 mins

MAKES 1 SERVINGS

INGREDIENTS

- ❖ ½ cup frozen and unsweetened blueberries
- ❖ ½ banana slices up
- ❖ ¾ cup plain nonfat Greek yogurt
- ❖ ¾ cup unsweetened vanilla almond milk
- ❖ 2 cups of ice cubes

INSTRUCTIONS

1. Add all of the ingredients into a blender. Blend until smooth.

Awesome Coffee with Butter

Prep Time: 5 mins **Cook Time:** 5 mins **Total Time:** 10 mins

MAKES 1 SERVINGS

INGREDIENTS

- ❖ 1 cup of water
- ❖ 1 tbsp coconut oil
- ❖ 1 tbsp unsalted butter
- ❖ 2 tbsp coffee

INSTRUCTIONS

1. Take a small pan, place it over medium heat, pour in water, and bring to boil.
2. Then add remaining ingredients, stir well, and cook until butter and oil have melted.
3. Remove pan from heat, pass the coffee through a strainer, and serve immediately.

Mediterranean Smoothie

Prep Time: 5 mins **Cook Time:** 5 mins **Total Time:** 10 mins

MAKES 2 SERVINGS

INGREDIENTS

- ❖ 2 cups of baby spinach
- ❖ 1 teaspoon fresh ginger root
- ❖ 1 frozen banana, pre-sliced
- ❖ 1 small mango
- ❖ ½ cup beet juice
- ❖ ½ cup of skim milk
- ❖ 4-6 ice cubes

INSTRUCTIONS

1. Take all ingredients and place them in your blender. Blend until thick and smooth. Serve.

Low Carb Green Smoothie

Prep Time: 15 mins **Cook Time:** 0 mins **Total Time:** 15 mins

MAKES 2 SERVINGS

INGREDIENTS

- ❖ 1/3 cup romaine lettuce
- ❖ 1/3 tablespoon fresh ginger, peeled and chopped
- ❖ 1½ cups filtered water
- ❖ 1/8 cup fresh pineapple, chopped
- ❖ ¾ tablespoon fresh parsley
- ❖ 1/3 cup raw cucumber, peeled and sliced
- ❖ ¼ Hass avocado
- ❖ ¼ cup kiwi fruit, peeled and chopped
- ❖ 1/3 tablespoon Swerve

INSTRUCTIONS

1. Put all the ingredients in a blender, then blend until smooth.
2. Pour into 2 serving glasses and serve chilled.

Strawberry-Rhubarb Smoothie

Prep Time: 5 mins **Cook Time:** 3 mins **Total Time:** 8 mins

MAKES 1 SERVING

INGREDIENTS

- ❖ 1 rhubarb stalk, chopped
- ❖ 1 cup sliced fresh strawberries
- ❖ ½ cup plain Greek yogurt
- ❖ 2 tablespoons honey Pinch ground cinnamon
- ❖ 3 ice cubes

INSTRUCTIONS

1. Place a small saucepan filled with water over high heat and bring to a boil. Add the rhubarb and boil for 3 minutes. Drain and transfer the rhubarb to a blender.

2. Add the strawberries, yogurt, honey, and cinnamon, and pulse the mixture until it is smooth.

Add the ice and blend until thick, with no ice lumps remaining. Pour the smoothie into a glass and enjoy cold.

Italian Breakfast Sausage with Baby Potatoes and Vegetables

Prep Time: 15 mins **Cook Time:** 30 mins **Total Time:** 45 mins

MAKES 4 SERVINGS

INGREDIENTS

- ❖ 1 lb. sweet Italian sausage links, sliced on the bias (diagonal)
- ❖ 2 cups baby potatoes, halved
- ❖ 2 cups broccoli florets
- ❖ 1 cup onions cut into 1-inch chunks
- ❖ 2 cups small mushrooms -half or quarter the large ones for uniform size
- ❖ 1 cup baby carrots
- ❖ 2 tbsp olive oil
- ❖ 1/2 tsp garlic powder

- ❖ 1/2 tsp Italian seasoning
- ❖ 1 tsp salt
- ❖ 1/2 tsp pepper

INSTRUCTIONS

1. Preheat the oven to 400 degrees F. In a large bowl, add the baby potatoes, broccoli florets, onions, small mushrooms, and baby carrots.
2. Add in the olive oil, salt, pepper, garlic powder, and Italian seasoning and toss to evenly coat, then spread the vegetables onto a sheet pan in one even layer.
3. Arrange the sausage slices on the pan over the vegetables. Bake for 30 minutes – make sure to sake halfway through to prevent sticking. Allow cooling.
4. Distribute the Italian sausages and vegetables among the containers and store them in the fridge for 2-3 days

Cheesy Thyme Waffles

Prep Time: 15 mins **Cook Time:** 5 mins **Total Time:** 20 mins

MAKES 2 SERVINGS

INGREDIENTS

- ❖ ½ cup mozzarella cheese, finely shredded
- ❖ ¼ cup Parmesan cheese
- ❖ ¼ large head cauliflower
- ❖ ½ cup collard greens 1 large egg
- ❖ 1 stalk green onion
- ❖ ½ tablespoon olive oil
- ❖ ½ teaspoon garlic powder
- ❖ ¼ teaspoon salt
- ❖ ½ tablespoon sesame seed
- ❖ 1 teaspoon fresh thyme, chopped
- ❖ ¼ teaspoon ground black pepper

<u>*INSTRUCTIONS*</u>

1. Put cauliflower, collard greens, spring onion, and thyme in a food processor, then pulse until smooth.
2. Dish out the mixture in a bowl and stir in the rest of the ingredients. Heat waffle iron and then transfer the mixture evenly over the griddle. Cook until a waffle is formed and dish out in a serving platter.

Mediterranean Breakfast Egg White Sandwich

Prep Time: 15 mins **Cook Time:** 30 mins **Total Time:** 45 mins

MAKES 1 SERVINGS

INGREDIENTS

- ❖ 1 tsp vegan butter
- ❖ ¼ cup egg whites
- ❖ 1 tsp chopped fresh herbs such as parsley, basil, rosemary
- ❖ 1 whole-grain seeded ciabatta roll
- ❖ 1 tbsp pesto
- ❖ 1-2 slices muenster cheese (or other cheese)
- ❖ About ½ cup roasted tomatoes
- ❖ Salt, to taste
- ❖ Pepper, to taste

Roasted Tomatoes:

- ❖ 10 oz grape tomatoes
- ❖ 1 tbsp extra virgin olive oil
- ❖ Kosher salt, to taste
- ❖ Coarse black pepper, to taste

INSTRUCTIONS

1. In a small nonstick skillet over medium heat, melt the vegan butter. Pour in egg whites, season with salt and pepper, sprinkle with fresh herbs, cook for 3-4 minutes or until the egg is done, flip once.
2. In the meantime, toast the ciabatta bread in a toaster. Once done, spread both halves with pesto.
3. Place the egg on the bottom half of the sandwich roll, folding if necessary, top with cheese, add the roasted tomatoes, and the top half of the rolled sandwich.
4. For the roasted tomatoes preheat the oven to 400 degrees F. Slice tomatoes in half lengthwise. Then place them onto a baking sheet and drizzle with the olive oil, toss to coat.

5. Season with salt and pepper and roast in the oven for about 20 minutes, until the skin appears wrinkled.

Ham Spinach Ballet

Prep Time: 30 mins **Cook Time:** 25 mins **Total Time:** 55 mins

MAKES 2 SERVINGS

INGREDIENTS

- ❖ 4 teaspoons cream
- ❖ ¾ pound fresh baby spinach
- ❖ 7-ounce ham, sliced
- ❖ Salt and black pepper, to taste
- ❖ 1 tablespoon unsalted butter, melted

INSTRUCTIONS

1. Preheat the oven to 360 degrees F. and grease 2 ramekins with butter. Put butter and spinach in a skillet and cook for about 3 minutes.
2. Add cooked spinach in the ramekins and top with ham slices, cream, salt, and black pepper.

3. Bake for about 25 minutes, then dish out to serve hot.
4. For meal prepping, you can refrigerate this ham spinach ballet for about 3 days wrapped in foil.

Blueberry Greek Yogurt Pancakes

Prep Time: 15 mins **Cook Time:** 15 mins **Total Time:** 30 mins

MAKES 6 SERVINGS

INGREDIENTS

- ❖ 1 1/4 cup all-purpose flour
- ❖ 2 tsp baking powder
- ❖ 1 tsp baking soda
- ❖ 1/4 tsp salt
- ❖ 1/4 cup sugar
- ❖ 3 eggs
- ❖ 3 tbsp vegan butter unsalted, melted
- ❖ 1/2 cup milk
- ❖ 1 1/2 cups Greek yogurt plain, non-fat
- ❖ 1/2 cup blueberries optional

Toppings:

❖ Greek yogurt
❖ Mixed berries – blueberries, raspberries, and blackberries

INSTRUCTIONS

1. In a large bowl, whisk together the flour, salt, baking powder, and baking soda. In a separate bowl, whisk together butter, sugar, eggs, Greek yogurt, and milk until the mixture is smooth.
2. Then add in the Greek yogurt mixture from step to the dry mixture in step 1, mix to combine, allow the batter to sit for 20 minutes to get a smooth texture – if using blueberries fold them into the pancake batter.
3. Heat the pancake griddle, spray with non-stick butter spray or just brush with butter. Pour the batter, in 1/4 cupfuls, onto the griddle.
4. Cook until the bubbles on top burst and create small holes, lift the corners of the pancake to see if they're golden brown on the bottom
5. With a wide spatula, flip the pancake and cook on the other side until lightly browned. Serve.

Coconut Porridge

Prep Time: 15 mins **Cook Time:** 0 mins **Total Time:** 15 mins

MAKES 6 SERVINGS

INGREDIENTS

❖ Powdered erythritol as needed

❖ 1 ½ cups almond milk, unsweetened

❖ 2 tablespoons vanilla protein powder

❖ 3 tablespoons Golden Flaxseed meal

❖ 2 tablespoons coconut flour

INSTRUCTIONS

1. Take a bowl and mix in a flaxseed meal, protein powder, coconut flour, and mix well. Add mix to the saucepan (placed over medium heat).

2. Add almond milk and stir, let the mixture thicken. Add your desired amount of sweetener, then serve. Enjoy!

Baked Oatmeal with Cinnamon

Prep Time: 10 mins **Cook Time:** 25 mins **Total Time:** 35 mins

MAKES 4 SERVINGS

INGREDIENTS

- ❖ 1 cup oatmeal
- ❖ 1/3 cup milk
- ❖ 1 pear, chopped
- ❖ 1 teaspoon vanilla extract
- ❖ 1 tablespoon Splenda
- ❖ 1 teaspoon butter
- ❖ ½ teaspoon ground cinnamon
- ❖ 1 egg, beaten

INSTRUCTIONS

1. In the big bowl mix up together oatmeal, milk, egg, vanilla extract, Splenda, and ground cinnamon.

2. Melt butter and add it to the oatmeal mixture. Then add chopped pear and stir it well.
3. Transfer the oatmeal mixture to the casserole mold and flatten gently. Cover it with foil and secure edges.
4. Bake the oatmeal for 25 minutes at 350F.

Mediterranean Feta and Quinoa Egg Muffins

Prep Time: 15 mins **Cook Time:** 15 mins **Total Time:** 30 mins

MAKES 12 SERVINGS

INGREDIENTS

- ❖ 2 cups baby spinach finely chopped
- ❖ 1 cup chopped or sliced cherry tomatoes
- ❖ 1/2 cup finely chopped onion
- ❖ 1 tablespoon chopped fresh oregano
- ❖ 1 cup crumbled feta cheese
- ❖ 1/2 cup chopped (pitted) kalamata olives
- ❖ 2 teaspoons high oleic sunflower oil
- ❖ 1 cup cooked quinoa
- ❖ 8 eggs
- ❖ 1/4 teaspoon salt

INSTRUCTIONS

1. Pre-heat oven to 350 degrees Fahrenheit, and then prepare 12 silicone muffin holders on the baking sheet, or just grease a 12-cup muffin tin with oil and set aside.

2. Finely chop the vegetables and then heat the skillet to medium. After that, add the vegetable oil and onions, then sauté for 2 minutes.

3. Then, add tomatoes and sauté for another minute, then add spinach and sauté until wilted, about 1 minute.

4. Place the beaten egg into a bowl and then add lots of vegetables like feta cheese, quinoa, veggie mixture as well as salt, and then stir well until everything is properly combined.

5. Pour the ready mixture into greased muffin tins or silicone cups, dividing the mixture equally. Then, bake it in an oven for 30 minutes or so.

Breakfast Spanakopita

Prep Time: 15 mins **Cook Time:** 1 hr **Total Time:** 1 hr 15 mins

MAKES 6 SERVINGS

INGREDIENTS

- ❖ 2 cups spinach
- ❖ 1 white onion, diced
- ❖ ½ cup fresh parsley
- ❖ 1 teaspoon minced garlic
- ❖ 3 oz Feta cheese, crumbled
- ❖ 1 teaspoon ground paprika
- ❖ 2 eggs, beaten
- ❖ 1/3 cup butter, melted
- ❖ 2 oz Phyllo dough

INSTRUCTIONS

1. Separate Phyllo dough into 2 parts.

2. Brush the casserole mold with butter well and place 1 part of Phyllo dough inside.
3. Brush its surface with butter too.
4. Put the spinach and fresh parsley in the blender. Blend it until smooth and transfer in the mixing bowl.
5. Add minced garlic, Feta cheese, ground paprika, eggs, and diced onion. Mix up well.
6. Place the spinach mixture in the casserole mold and flatten it well.
7. Cover the spinach mixture with the remaining Phyllo dough and pour the remaining butter over it.
8. Bake spanakopita for 1 hour at 350F. Cut it into servings.

Full Eggs in a Squash

Prep Time: 15 mins **Cook Time:** 20 mins **Total Time:** 35 mins

MAKES 5 SERVINGS

INGREDIENTS

- ❖ 1 acorn squash
- ❖ 6 whole eggs
- ❖ 2 tablespoons extra virgin olive oil
- ❖ Salt and pepper as needed
- ❖ 5-6 pitted dates
- ❖ 8 walnut halves
- ❖ A fresh bunch of parsley

INSTRUCTIONS

1. Pre-heat your oven to 375 degrees Fahrenheit. Slice squash crosswise and prepare 3 slices with

holes. While slicing the squash, make sure that each slice has a measurement of ¾ inch thickness.

2. Remove the seeds from the slices. Line a baking sheet with parchment paper. Transfer the slices to your baking sheet and season them with salt and pepper.

3. Bake in your oven for 20 minutes. Chop the walnuts and dates on your cutting board. Take the baking dish out of the oven and drizzle slices with olive oil.

4. Crack an egg into each of the holes in the slices and season with pepper and salt. Sprinkle the chopped walnuts on top. Bake for 10 minutes more. Garnish with parsley and add maple syrup.

Overnight Oats with Nuts

Prep Time: 10 mins **Cook Time:** 8 hr **Total Time:** 8 hr 10 mins

MAKES 2 SERVINGS

INGREDIENTS

- ❖ ½ cup oats
- ❖ 2 teaspoons chia seeds, dried
- ❖ 1 tablespoon almond, chopped
- ❖ ½ teaspoon walnuts, chopped 1 cup skim milk
- ❖ 2 teaspoons honey
- ❖ ½ teaspoon vanilla extract

INSTRUCTIONS

1. In the big bowl mix up together chia seeds, oats, honey, and vanilla extract. Then add skim milk, walnuts, and almonds. Stir well.

2. Transfer the prepared mixture into the mason jars and close with lids. Put the mason jars in the fridge and leave them overnight.

3. Store the meal in the fridge for up to 2 days.

Crumbled Feta and Scallions

Prep Time: 5 mins **Cook Time:** 15 mins **Total Time:** 20 mins

MAKES 12 SERVINGS

INGREDIENTS

- ❖ 2 tablespoons of unsalted butter (replace with canola oil for full effect)
- ❖ ½ cup of chopped up scallions
- ❖ 1 cup of crumbled feta cheese
- ❖ 8 large-sized eggs
- ❖ 2/3 cup of milk
- ❖ ½ teaspoon of dried Italian seasoning
- ❖ Salt as needed
- ❖ Freshly ground black pepper as needed
- ❖ Cooking oil spray

INSTRUCTIONS

1. Pre-heat your oven to 400 degrees Fahrenheit. Take a 3-4 ounce muffin pan and grease with cooking oil. Take a non-stick pan and place it over medium heat.

2. Add butter and allow the butter to melt. Add half of the scallions and stir fry. Keep them to the side. Take a medium-sized bowl and add eggs, Italian seasoning, and milk and whisk well.

3. Add the stir-fried scallions and feta cheese and mix. Season with pepper and salt. Pour the mix into the muffin tin. Transfer the muffin tin to your oven and bake for 15 minutes. Serve with a sprinkle of scallions.

Rocket Tomatoes and Mushroom Frittata

Prep Time: 5 mins **Cook Time:** 15 mins **Total Time:** 20 mins

MAKES 4 SERVINGS

INGREDIENTS

- ❖ 2 tablespoons of butter (replace with canola oil for full effect)
- ❖ 1 chopped up medium-sized onion
- ❖ 2 minced cloves of garlic
- ❖ 1 cup of coarsely chopped baby rocket tomato
- ❖ 1 cup of sliced button mushrooms
- ❖ 6 large pieces of eggs
- ❖ ½ cup of skim milk
- ❖ 1 teaspoon of dried rosemary
- ❖ Salt as needed

❖ Ground black pepper as needed

INSTRUCTIONS

1. Pre-heat your oven to 400 degrees Fahrenheit. Take a large oven-proof pan and place it over medium heat. Heat some oil.
2. Stir fry your garlic, onion for about 2 minutes. Add the mushroom, rosemary, and rockets and cook for 3 minutes. Take a medium-sized bowl and beat your eggs alongside the milk.
3. Season it with some salt and pepper. Pour the egg mixture into your pan with the vegetables and sprinkle some Parmesan.
4. Reduce the heat to low and cover with the lid. Let it cook for 3 minutes. Transfer the pan into your oven and bake for 10 minutes until fully settled.
5. Reduce the heat to low and cover with your lid. Let it cook for 3 minutes. Transfer the pan into your oven and then bake for another 10 minutes. Serve hot.

St. Valentine's Mediterranean Pancakes

Prep Time: 10 mins **Cook Time:** 20 mins **Total Time:** 30 mins

MAKES 2 SERVINGS

INGREDIENTS

- ❖ 4 eggs, preferably organic
- ❖ 2 pieces banana, peeled and then cut into small pieces
- ❖ 1/2 teaspoon extra-virgin olive oil (for the pancake pan)
- ❖ 1 tablespoon milled flax seeds, preferably organic
- ❖ 1 tablespoon bee pollen, milled, preferably organic

45

INSTRUCTIONS

1. Crack the eggs into a mixing bowl. Add in the banana, flax seeds, and bee pollen. With a hand mixer, blend the ingredients until the smooth batter in texture.
2. Put a few drops of olive oil in a nonstick pancake pan over medium flame or heat. Pour some batter into the pan; cook for about 2 minutes, undisturbed until the bottom of the pancake is golden and can be lifted easily from the pan. With a silicone spatula, lift and flip the pancake; cook for about 30seconds more and transfer into a plate.
3. Repeat the process with the remaining batter, oiling the pan with every new batter.
4. Serve the pancake as you cook or serve them all together topped with vanilla, strawberry, pine nuts jam.

Blueberries Quinoa

Prep Time: 5 mins **Cook Time:** 0 mins **Total Time:** 5 mins

MAKES 4 SERVINGS

INGREDIENTS

- ❖ 2 cups almond milk
- ❖ 2 cups quinoa, already cooked
- ❖ ½ tsp cinnamon powder
- ❖ 1 tbsp. honey
- ❖ 1 cup blueberries
- ❖ ¼ cup walnuts, chopped

INSTRUCTIONS

1. In a bowl, mix the quinoa with the milk and the rest of the ingredients, toss, divide into smaller bowls and serve for breakfast.

Eggless Spinach and Bacon Quiche

Prep Time: 10 mins **Cook Time:** 20 mins **Total Time:** 30 mins

MAKES 8 SERVINGS

INGREDIENTS

- ❖ 1 cup fresh spinach, chopped
- ❖ 4 slices of bacon, cooked and chopped
- ❖ ½ cup mozzarella cheese, shredded
- ❖ 4 tablespoons milk
- ❖ 4 dashes of Tabasco sauce
- ❖ 1 cup Parmesan cheese, shredded
- ❖ Salt and freshly ground black pepper, to taste

INSTRUCTIONS

1. Preheat the Airfryer to 325 degrees F and grease a baking dish. Put all the ingredients in a bowl, then mix well.
2. Transfer the mixture into a prepared baking dish and cook for about 8 minutes. Dish out and serve.

Minestrone Chickpeas and Macaroni Casserole

Prep Time: 15 mins **Cook Time:** 7 hr 25 mins **Total Time:** 7 hr 40 mins

MAKES 5 SERVINGS

INGREDIENTS

- ❖ 1 (15-ounce / 425-g) can chickpeas, drained and rinsed
- ❖ 1 (28-ounce / 794-g) can diced tomatoes, with the juice
- ❖ 1 (6-ounce / 170-g) can no-salt-added tomato paste
- ❖ 3 medium carrots, sliced
- ❖ 3 cloves garlic, minced
- ❖ 1 medium yellow onion, chopped
- ❖ 1 cup low-sodium vegetable soup

- ❖ ½ teaspoon dried rosemary
- ❖ 1 teaspoon dried oregano
- ❖ 2 teaspoons maple syrup
- ❖ ½ teaspoon sea salt
- ❖ ¼ teaspoon ground black pepper
- ❖ ½ pound (227-g) fresh green beans, trimmed and cut into bite-size pieces
- ❖ 1 cup macaroni pasta
- ❖ 2 ounces (57 g) Parmesan cheese, grated

INSTRUCTIONS

1. Except for the green beans, pasta, and Parmesan cheese, combine all the ingredients in the slow cooker and stir to mix well. Put the slow cooker lid on and cook on low for 7 hours.
2. Fold in the pasta and green beans. Put the lid on and cook on high for 20 minutes or until the vegetable are soft and the pasta is al dente.
3. Pour them in a large serving bowl and spread them with Parmesan cheese before serving.

Lentil Salmon Salad

Prep Time: 5 mins **Cook Time:** 20 mins **Total Time:** 25 mins

MAKES 4 SERVINGS

INGREDIENTS

- ❖ Vegetable stock - 2 cups
- ❖ Green lentils - 1, rinsed
- ❖ Red onion - 1, chopped
- ❖ Parsley - 1 2 cup, chopped
- ❖ Smoked salmon - 4 oz., shredded
- ❖ Cilantro - 2 tbsp., chopped
- ❖ Red pepper - 1, chopped
- ❖ Lemon - 1, juiced
- ❖ Salt and pepper - to taste

<u>INSTRUCTIONS</u>

1. Cook vegetable stock and lentils in a saucepan for 15 to 20 minutes, on low heat. Ensure all liquid has been absorbed and then remove from heat.
2. Pour into a salad bowl and top with red pepper, parsley, cilantro, and salt and pepper (to suit your taste) and mix.
3. Mix in lemon juice and shredded salmon. This salad should be served fresh.

Lemon-Herbs Orzo

Prep Time: 15 mins **Cook Time:** 10 mins **Total Time:** 25 mins

MAKES 4 SERVINGS

INGREDIENTS

Orzo:

- ❖ 2 cups orzo
- ❖ ½ cup fresh basil, finely chopped
- ❖ 2 tablespoons lemon zest
- ❖ ½ cup fresh parsley, finely chopped

Dressing:

- ❖ ½ cup extra-virgin olive oil
- ❖ 1/3 cup lemon juice
- ❖ 1 teaspoon salt
- ❖ ½ teaspoon freshly ground black pepper

INSTRUCTIONS

1. Put the orzo in a large saucepan of boiling water and allow to cook for 6 minutes. Drain the orzo in a sieve and rinse well under cold running water. Set aside to cool completely.
2. When cooled, place the orzo in a large bowl. Mix in the basil, lemon zest, and parsley. Set aside.
3. Make the dressing: In a separate bowl, combine the olive oil, lemon juice, salt, and pepper. Stir to incorporate.
4. Pour the dressing into the bowl of orzo mixture and toss gently until everything is well combined. Serve immediately, or refrigerate for later.

Peppy Pepper Tomato Salad

Prep Time: 20 mins **Cook Time:** 10 mins **Total Time:** 30 mins

MAKES 4 SERVINGS

INGREDIENTS

- ❖ Yellow bell pepper - 1, cored and diced
- ❖ Cucumbers - 4, diced
- ❖ Red onion - 1, chopped
- ❖ Balsamic vinegar – 1 tbsp.
- ❖ Extra virgin olive oil – 2 tbsp.
- ❖ Tomatoes - 4, diced
- ❖ Red bell peppers - 2, cored and diced
- ❖ Chili flakes - 1 pinch
- ❖ Salt and pepper - to taste

**INSTRUCTIONS**

1. Mix all the above ingredients in a salad bowl, except salt and pepper. Season with salt and pepper to suit your taste and mix well.
2. Eat while fresh.

Bean and Toasted Pita Salad

Prep Time: 15 mins **Cook Time:** 6 mins **Total Time:** 21 mins

MAKES 4 SERVINGS

INGREDIENTS

- ❖ 3 tbsp chopped fresh mint
- ❖ 3 tbsp chopped fresh parsley
- ❖ 1 cup crumbled feta cheese
- ❖ 1 cup sliced romaine lettuce
- ❖ ½ cucumber, peeled and sliced
- ❖ 1 cup diced plum tomatoes
- ❖ 2 cups cooked pinto beans, well-drained and slightly warmed
- ❖ Pepper to taste
- ❖ 3 tbsp extra virgin olive oil
- ❖ 2 tbsp ground toasted cumin seeds

- ❖ 2 tbsp fresh lemon juice
- ❖ 1/8 tsp salt
- ❖ 2 cloves garlic, peeled
- ❖ 2 6-inch whole-wheat pita bread, cut or torn into bite-sized pieces

INSTRUCTIONS

1. On a large baking sheet, spread torn pita bread and bake in a preheated
2. 400F oven for 6 minutes. With the back of a knife, mash garlic and salt until paste-like. Add into a medium bowl.
3. Whisk in ground cumin and lemon juice. In a steady and slow stream, pour oil as you whisk continuously. Season with pepper.
4. In a large salad bowl, mix cucumber, tomatoes, and beans. Pour in dressing, toss to coat well. Add mint, parsley, feta, lettuce, and toasted pita, toss to mix once again, and serve.

Sweet and Sour Spinach Salad

Prep Time: 15 mins **Cook Time:** 0 mins **Total Time:** 15 mins

MAKES 4 SERVINGS

INGREDIENTS

- ❖ Red onions - 2, sliced
- ❖ Baby spinach leaves - 4
- ❖ Sesame oil - 1 2 tsp.
- ❖ Apple cider vinegar - 2 tbsp.
- ❖ Honey - 1 tsp.
- ❖ Sesame seeds - 2 tbsp.
- ❖ Salt and pepper

INSTRUCTIONS

1. Mix honey, sesame oil, vinegar, and sesame seeds in a small bowl to make a dressing. Add in salt and pepper to taste.

2. Add red onions and spinach together in a salad bowl.

3. Pour dressing over the salad and serve while cool and fresh.

Chickpea Fried Eggplant Salad

Prep Time: 15 mins **Cook Time:** 12 mins **Total Time:** 27 mins

MAKES 4 SERVINGS

INGREDIENTS

- ❖ 1 cup chopped dill
- ❖ 1 cup chopped parsley
- ❖ 1 cup cooked or canned chickpeas, drained
- ❖ 1 large eggplant, thinly sliced (no more than 1/4 inch in thickness)
- ❖ 1 small red onion, sliced in 1/2 moons
- ❖ 1/2 English cucumber, diced
- ❖ 3 Roma tomatoes, diced
- ❖ 3 tbsp Za'atar spice, divided
- ❖ oil for frying, preferably extra virgin olive oil
- ❖ Salt

Garlic Vinaigrette Ingredients:

- ❖ 1 large lime, juice of
- ❖ 1/3 cup extra virgin olive oil
- ❖ 1–2 garlic cloves, minced
- ❖ Salt & Pepper to taste

INSTRUCTIONS

1. On a baking sheet, spread out sliced eggplant and season with salt generously. Let it sit for 30 minutes. Then pat dry with a paper towel.
2. Place a small pot on medium-high fire and fill halfway with oil. Heat oil for 5 minutes. Fry eggplant in batches until golden brown, around 3 minutes per side.
3. Place cooked eggplants on a paper towel-lined plate. Once eggplants have cooled, assemble the eggplant on a serving dish. Sprinkle with 1 tbsp of Za'atar.
4. Mix dill, parsley, red onions, chickpeas, cucumbers, and tomatoes
5. In a large salad bowl. Sprinkle remaining Za'atar and gently toss to mix.
6. Whisk well the vinaigrette ingredients in a small bowl. Drizzle 2 tbsp of the dressing over the

fried eggplant. Add remaining dressing over the chickpea salad and mix.

7. Add the chickpea salad to the serving dish with the fried eggplant. Serve and enjoy.

Feta and Roasted Red Pepper Bruschetta

Prep Time: 15 mins **Cook Time:** 15 mins **Total Time:** 30 mins

MAKES 24 SERVINGS

INGREDIENTS

- ❖ 6 Kalamata olives, pitted, chopped
- ❖ 2 tablespoons green onion, minced
- ❖ 1/4 cup Parmesan cheese, grated, divided
- ❖ 1/4 cup extra-virgin olive oil brushing, or as needed
- ❖ 1/4 cup cherry tomatoes, thinly sliced
- ❖ 1 teaspoon lemon juice
- ❖ 1 tablespoon extra-virgin olive oil
- ❖ 1 tablespoon basil pesto
- ❖ 1 red bell pepper, halved, seeded

- ❖ 1 piece (12 inches) whole-wheat baguette, cut into
- ❖ 1/2-inch thick slices
- ❖ 1 package (4 ounces) feta cheese with basil and sun-dried tomatoes, crumbled
- ❖ 1 clove garlic, minced

INSTRUCTIONS

1. Preheat the oven broiler. Place the oven rack 6 inches from the heat source. Brush both sides of the baguette slices, with the 1/4 cup olive oil. Arrange the bread slices on a baking sheet; toast for about 1 minute on each side, carefully watching to avoid burning. Remove the toasted slices, transferring them to another baking sheet.

2. With the cut sides down, place the red peppers in a baking sheet; broil for about 8 to 10 minutes or until the skin is charred and blistered. Transfer the roasted peppers into a bowl; cover with plastic wrap. Let cool, remove the charred skin. Discard skin and chop the roasted peppers.

3. In a bowl, mix the roasted red peppers, cherry tomatoes, feta cheese, green onion, olives, pesto, 1 tablespoon olive oil, garlic, and lemon juice.

4. Top each bread with 1 tablespoon of the roasted pepper mix, sprinkle lightly with the Parmesan cheese.

5. Return the baking sheet with the topped bruschetta; broil for about 1-2 minutes or until the topping is lightly browned.

White Bean Soup

Prep Time: 10 mins **Cook Time:** 35 mins **Total Time:** 45 mins

MAKES 2 SERVINGS

INGREDIENTS

- ❖ 1 tablespoon virgin olive oil
- ❖ 1 red onion (chopped)
- ❖ 1 garlic clove (minced)
- ❖ 1 celery stalk (chopped)
- ❖ 1 cup spinach (fresh, finely chopped)
- ❖ 1 tablespoon lemon juice (fresh squeezed)
- ❖ 2x 16-ounce cans white kidney beans (drained, rinsed)
- ❖ 2 cups chicken broth (or a 14-ounce can of low-sodium chicken broth)
- ❖ ¼ teaspoon thyme (dried)
- ❖ ½ teaspoon black pepper 1 ½ cups water

68

INSTRUCTIONS

1. Place a large saucepan on your stove. Add the virgin olive oil to your pan and turn the heat to medium-high. Add the celery, chopped onions, and minced garlic to the pan and allow them to cook for 5 minutes.

2. Add the white kidney beans, chicken broth, water, thyme, and black pepper to the saucepan.

3. Allow the liquid to come to a boil, then reduce heat to medium-low and let the soup simmer for 15 minutes.

4. Transfer two cups of the bean and vegetables from the saucepan to a bowl. Use a slotted spoon to get as little of the liquid as possible. Set the bowl to the side.

5. Use an emulsion blender to blend the remaining soup mixture in the saucepan. You want to get a nice smooth consistency.

6. If you do not have an emulsion blender you can use a regular stand-alone blender. Just work in batches to blend everything. Once everything has been thoroughly blended, return to your saucepan.

7. Add the 2 cups of beans and vegetable mixture that you removed earlier back into the soup. Bring the soup back up to a boil, stirring occasionally.

8. Add the spinach to the soup; after 2 minutes it should begin to wilt.

9. Turn the heat all the way off, and then stirs in the lemon juice just before serving.

Mediterranean Polenta Cups Recipe

Prep Time: 10 mins **Cook Time:** 10 mins **Total Time:** 20 mins

MAKES 24 SERVINGS

INGREDIENTS

- ❖ 1 cup yellow cornmeal 1 garlic clove, minced
- ❖ 1/2 teaspoon fresh thyme, minced or 1/4 teaspoon dried thyme
- ❖ 1/2 teaspoon salt
- ❖ 1/4 cup feta cheese, crumbled
- ❖ 1/4 teaspoon pepper
- ❖ 2 tablespoons fresh basil, chopped
- ❖ 4 cups water
- ❖ 4 plum tomatoes, finely chopped

INSTRUCTIONS

1. In a heavy, large saucepan, bring the water and the salt to a boil; reduce the heat to a gentle boil. Slowly whisk in the cornmeal; cook, stirring with a wooden spoon for about 15 to 20 minutes, or until the polenta is thick and pulls away cleanly from the sides of the pan. Remove from the heat; stir in the pepper and the thyme.

2. Grease miniature muffin cups with cooking spray. Spoon a heaping tablespoon of the polenta mixture into each muffin cup.

3. With the back of a spoon, make an indentation in the center of each; cover and chill until the mixture is set.

4. Meanwhile, combine the feta cheese, tomatoes, garlic, and basil in a small-sized bowl.

5. Unmold the chilled polenta cups; place them on an ungreased baking sheet. Tops each indentation with 1 heaping tablespoon of the feta mixture. Broil the cups 4 inches from the heat source for about 5 to 7 minutes, or until heated through.

Braised Lamb Shanks with Veggies

Prep Time: 15 mins **Cook Time:** 30 mins **Total Time:** 45 mins

MAKES 6 SERVINGS

INGREDIENTS

- ❖ 6 lamb shanks
- ❖ 1 onion, chopped
- ❖ 1 lb. frozen carrots and potatoes, chopped
- ❖ Seasoning mixture (2 1/4 teaspoons garlic powder, 1 teaspoon sweet Spanish paprika and 3/4 teaspoon ground nutmeg)
- ❖ 28 oz. canned tomatoes with juice

INSTRUCTIONS

1. Season the lamb shanks with the seasoning mixture. Pour 2 tablespoons olive oil into the Instant Pot. Set it to sauté.

2. Brown the lamb shanks for 8 minutes. Add the rest of the ingredients. Mix well. Cover the pot. Set it to manual. Cook at high pressure for 20 minutes. Release the pressure naturally.

Chopped Chicken on Greek Salad

Prep Time: 10 mins **Cook Time:** 0 mins **Total Time:** 10 mins

MAKES 4 SERVINGS

INGREDIENTS

- ❖ ¼ tsp pepper
- ❖ ¼ tsp salt
- ❖ ½ cup crumbled feta cheese
- ❖ ½ cup finely chopped red onion
- ❖ ½ cup sliced ripe black olives
- ❖ 1 medium cucumber, peeled, seeded, and chopped
- ❖ 1 tbsp chopped fresh dill
- ❖ 1 tsp garlic powder
- ❖ 1/3 cup red wine vinegar
- ❖ 2 ½ cups chopped cooked chicken
- ❖ 2 medium tomatoes, chopped

❖ 2 tbsp extra virgin olive oil

❖ 6 cups chopped romaine lettuce

INSTRUCTIONS

1. In a large bowl, whisk well pepper, salt, garlic powder, dill, oil, and vinegar. Add feta, olives, onion, cucumber, tomatoes, chicken, and lettuce.

2. Toss well to combine. Serve and enjoy.

Rolled Up Tender Beef

Prep Time: 15 mins **Cook Time:** 20 mins **Total Time:** 35 mins

MAKES 4 SERVINGS

INGREDIENTS

- ❖ 2 lbs. beef flank steak
- ❖ 2 tablespoons unsalted butter
- ❖ 4 tablespoons pesto
- ❖ 6 slices cheddar cheese
- ❖ ½ cup fresh baby spinach
- ❖ Salt and black pepper to taste
- ❖ 1 tablespoon olive oil

INSTRUCTIONS

1. Spread the butter over the steak. Then cover with pesto. Layer the cheese slices, baby spinach, and season with salt and pepper. Roll

up the meat and secure it with toothpicks. Season with salt and pepper.

2. Preheat your air fryer to 390°Fahrenheit. Sprinkle inside of the basket with olive oil. Cook for 20- minutes.

3. Slice beef roll and serve.

Jerk-Style Chicken Wings

Prep Time: 10 mins **Cook Time:** 20 mins **Total Time:** 30 mins

MAKES 5 SERVINGS

INGREDIENTS

- ❖ 3 lbs. chicken wings
- ❖ 2 tablespoons olive oil
- ❖ 1 tablespoon fresh thyme, finely chopped
- ❖ 1 teaspoon liquid Stevia
- ❖ Pinch of white pepper
- ❖ Pinch of cayenne pepper
- ❖ Pinch of allspice
- ❖ 1 habanero pepper, deseeded and chopped
- ❖ 6 cloves garlic, finely chopped
- ❖ 2 tablespoons soy sauce
- ❖ 1 tablespoon fresh ginger, finely grated
- ❖ 4 scallions, chopped

- ❖ 5 tablespoons lime juice
- ❖ ½ cup red wine vinegar
- ❖ Salt to taste

INSTRUCTIONS

1. Prepare the marinade in a bowl, mix all the ingredients, excluding the chicken. Season with salt. Mix marinade and chicken wings in a zip-lock bag, seal the bag and shake to mix contents. Marinate in the fridge for 2- hours.
2. Preheat your air fryer to 350°Fahrenheit. Drain the marinated chicken wings on a paper towel-lined baking sheet and pat dry with more paper towels.
3. Place the chicken inside of air fryer and cook for 10-minutes. Flip over chicken wings and cook for an additional 10-minutes.

Herb Roasted Pork

Prep Time: 20 mins **Cook Time:** 2 hr **Total Time:** 2 hr 20 mins

MAKES 10 SERVINGS

INGREDIENTS

- ❖ 5 and ½ pounds pork loin roast, trimmed, chine bone removed
- ❖ Salt and black pepper to taste
- ❖ 3 garlic cloves, minced
- ❖ 2 tablespoons rosemary, chopped
- ❖ 1 teaspoon fennel, ground
- ❖ 1 tablespoon fennel seeds
- ❖ 2 teaspoons red pepper, crushed
- ❖ ¼ cup olive oil

INSTRUCTIONS

1. In a food processor mix garlic with fennel seeds, fennel, rosemary, red pepper, some black

pepper, and olive oil and blend until you obtain a paste.

2. Place pork roast in a roasting pan, spread 2 tablespoons garlic paste all over, and rub well. Season with salt and pepper, place in the oven at 400 degrees F, and bake for 1 hour.

3. Reduce heat to 325 degrees F and bake for another 35 minutes. Carve roast into chops, divide between plates, and serve right away.

Calamari with Tomato Sauce

Prep Time: 8 mins **Cook Time:** 10 mins **Total Time:** 18 mins

MAKES 4 SERVINGS

INGREDIENTS

- ❖ 3 lbs. calamari
- ❖ 1/3 cup olive oil
- ❖ 1 tablespoon fresh oregano
- ❖ 1 teaspoon lemon juice
- ❖ 1 tablespoon garlic, minced
- ❖ ¼ teaspoon chopped fresh lemon peel
- ❖ ¼ teaspoon crushed red pepper
- ❖ ¼ cup vinegar

Sauce:

- ❖ 1 lb. fresh whole tomatoes

- ❖ 3 cloves garlic, minced
- ❖ 1 stalk of celery, chopped
- ❖ 1 tablespoon olive oil
- ❖ ½ green bell pepper
- ❖ Salt and pepper to taste
- ❖ ½ cup onion, chopped

INSTRUCTIONS

1. To make the sauce, mix all the sauce ingredients and add them to the blender. Blend until the mixture is smooth. Clean the calamari and slice it into ½-inch rings. Season calamari with vinegar, red pepper, lemon peel, garlic, lemon juice, and oregano.
2. Add oil to the air fryer. Add calamari with its juice. Air fry for about 6-minutes. Stir once and air fry for another 2-minutes. Serve hot with sauce.

Orange Fish Meal

Prep Time: 10 mins **Cook Time:** 5 mins **Total Time:** 15 mins

MAKES 4 SERVINGS

INGREDIENTS

- ❖ ¼ teaspoon kosher or sea salt
- ❖ 1 tablespoon extra-virgin olive oil
- ❖ 1 tablespoon orange juice
- ❖ 4 (4-ounce) tilapia fillets, with or without skin
- ❖ ¼ cup chopped red onion
- ❖ 1 avocado, pitted, skinned, and sliced

INSTRUCTIONS

1. Take a baking dish of 9-inch; add olive oil, orange juice, and salt. Mix well. Add fish fillets and coat well. Add onions over fish fillets.

2. Cover with plastic wrap. Microwave for 3 minutes until fish is cooked well and easy to flake. Serve warm with sliced avocado on top.

Salt and Pepper Calamari and Scallops

Prep Time: 15 mins **Cook Time:** 10 mins **Total Time:** 25 mins

MAKES 4 SERVINGS

INGREDIENTS

- ❖ 8 ounces (227 g) calamari steaks, cut into ½-inch-thick rings
- ❖ 8 ounces (227 g) sea scallops
- ❖ 1½ teaspoons salt, divided
- ❖ 1 teaspoon garlic powder
- ❖ 1 teaspoon freshly ground black pepper
- ❖ 1/3 cup extra-virgin olive oil
- ❖ 2 tablespoons almond butter

INSTRUCTIONS

1. Place the calamari and scallops on several layers

of paper towels and pat dry. Sprinkle with 1 teaspoon of salt and allow to sit for 15 minutes at room temperature.

2. Pat dry with additional paper towels. Sprinkle with pepper and garlic powder. In a deep medium skillet, heat the olive oil and butter over medium-high heat.

3. When the oil is hot but not smoking, add the scallops and calamari in a single layer to the skillet and sprinkle with the remaining ½ teaspoon of salt.

4. Cook for 2 to 4 minutes on each side, depending on the size of the scallops, until just golden but still slightly opaque in the center.

5. Using a slotted spoon, remove from the skillet and transfer to a serving platter. Allow the cooking oil to cool slightly and drizzle over the seafood before serving.

Breaded Fish

Prep Time: 5 mins **Cook Time:** 12 mins **Total Time:** 17 mins

MAKES 4 SERVINGS

INGREDIENTS

- ❖ 4 fish fillets
- ❖ 1 egg
- ❖ 5-ounces breadcrumbs
- ❖ 4 tablespoons olive oil

INSTRUCTIONS

1. Preheat your air fryer to 350°Fahrenheit. In a bowl mix oil and breadcrumbs. Whisk egg. Gently dip the fish into the egg and then into the crumb mixture.
2. Put into the air fryer and cook for 12-minutes.

Air-Fried Crab Herb Croquettes

Prep Time: 10 mins **Cook Time:** 18 mins **Total Time:** 28 mins

MAKES 6 SERVINGS

INGREDIENTS

- ❖ 1 lb. crab meat
- ❖ 1 cup breadcrumbs
- ❖ 2 egg whites
- ❖ Salt and black pepper to taste
- ❖ ½ teaspoon parsley, chopped
- ❖ ¼ teaspoon chives
- ❖ ¼ teaspoon tarragon
- ❖ 2 tablespoon celeries, chopped
- ❖ 4 tablespoon mayonnaise
- ❖ 4 tablespoons light sour cream
- ❖ 1 teaspoon olive oil

- ½ teaspoon lime juice
- ½ cup red pepper, chopped
- ¼ cup onion, chopped

INSTRUCTIONS

1. Preheat your air fryer to 355°Fahrenheit. Add breadcrumbs with salt and pepper in a bowl. In another small bowl add the eggs. Add all the remaining ingredients into another bowl and mix well. Make croquettes from crab mixture and dip into egg whites, and then into breadcrumbs.

2. Place into the air fryer and cook for 18-minutes.

Apple Pie Bread Pudding with Pecans

Prep Time: 10 mins **Cook Time:** 28 mins **Total Time:** 38 mins

MAKES 8 SERVINGS

INGREDIENTS

- ❖ 4 Granny Smith apples, peeled and chopped
- ❖ 2 large eggs, whisked
- ❖ 1/3 cup pecans, chopped
- ❖ 1 1/3 cup milk
- ❖ 7 small-sized slices of sweet bread, torn into pieces
- ❖ 1 teaspoon apple pie spice
- ❖ 1 ½ tablespoons butter, softened
- ❖ 2 tablespoons cornstarch
- ❖ 2 tablespoons Truvia for baking

INSTRUCTIONS

1. Take two mixing bowls. In the first bowl, add the bread pieces. In the second bowl, mix milk, egg, and apple pie spice. Scrap milk/egg mixture into the first dish with sweetbread pieces. Allow to soak for 10-minutes; press with a wide spatula.

2. Meanwhile, combine the apples, Truvia, and cornstarch. Place over the bread mixture. Drizzle melted butter over the top; top with chopped pecans.

3. Evenly divide the bread pudding mixture among 2 mini loaf pans. Bake in preheated air-fryer for 28-minutes at 315°Fahrenheit.

Quinoa Granola

Prep Time: 15 mins **Cook Time:** 35 mins **Total Time:** 50 mins

MAKES 7 SERVINGS

INGREDIENTS

* ❖ 1 cup old fashioned rolled oats
* ❖ 2 cups raw almonds, chopped
* ❖ ½ cup white quinoa, uncooked
* ❖ 1 tablespoon coconut sugar
* ❖ 3 ½ tablespoon coconut oil
* ❖ ¼ cup maple syrup pinch sea salt

INSTRUCTIONS

1. Preheat the oven to 340F. Add quinoa, oats, almonds, sugar, and salt to a bowl. Mix well. Add maple syrup and coconut oil to a pan. Heat over

medium heat for 3 minutes, whisking along.

2. Add dry ingredients and stir to coat well. Place on a baking sheet and spread. Bake for 20 minutes. Remove from the oven, then toss the granola.

3. Turn the pan around and bake for 8 minutes more. Cool completely and serve.

Creamed Peach and Almond Dessert

Prep Time: 10 mins **Cook Time:** 38 mins **Total Time:** 48 mins

MAKES 6 SERVINGS

INGREDIENTS

- ❖ 6 peaches, pitted and halved
- ❖ 1/3 almonds, chopped
- ❖ Well-chilled heavy cream to serve
- ❖ 1 teaspoon pure vanilla extract
- ❖ Coconut oil spray for pan
- ❖ 2 tablespoons Truvia for baking
- ❖ 1 teaspoon candied ginger

INSTRUCTIONS

1. Firstly, spray a baking pan with coconut oil spray; lower the peaches onto the bottom of the pan. In

a bowl, combine almonds, Truvia, vanilla, candied ginger. Scrape this mixture into the baking dish over the peaches.

2. Bake at 380°Fahrenheit for 38-minutes. Garnish dessert with heavy cream.

Fig Smoothie with Cinnamon

Prep Time: 5 mins **Cook Time:** 0 mins **Total Time:** 5 mins

MAKES 1 SERVINGS

INGREDIENTS

- ❖ 1 large ripe fig
- ❖ 3 dessertspoons porridge oats
- ❖ 3 rounded dessertspoons Greek yogurt
- ❖ ½ teaspoon ground cinnamon 200 ml orange juice
- ❖ 3 ice cubes

INSTRUCTIONS

1. Wash and dry the fig. Chop. Add all ingredients to a blender. Blend well. Serve.

Cranberry Pound Cake

Prep Time: 10 mins **Cook Time:** 20 mins **Total Time:** 30 mins

MAKES 8 SERVINGS

INGREDIENTS

- ❖ 1 cup almond flour
- ❖ 1/3 teaspoon baking soda
- ❖ 1/3 teaspoon baking powder
- ❖ 1 tablespoon Truvia for baking
- ❖ ½ teaspoon ground cloves
- ❖ ½ cup cranberries, fresh or thawed
- ❖ 2 eggs plus 1 egg yolk, beaten
- ❖ ½ teaspoon vanilla paste
- ❖ 1 stick butter
- ❖ ½ teaspoon cardamom
- ❖ 1/3 teaspoon ground cinnamon
- ❖ 1 tablespoon browned butter

INSTRUCTIONS

1. Preheat your air-fryer to 355°Fahrenheit. In a bowl, combine the flour with baking soda, baking powder, Truvia, ground cloves, cinnamon, and cardamom.
2. In another bowl, add a stick of butter, vanilla paste, mix in the eggs and whisk until light and fluffy. Add the flour/sweetener mixture to butter/egg mixture and fold in cranberries and browned butter. Add the mixture into a greased cake pan.
3. Bake in preheated air-fryer for 20-minutes.

Savory Feta Spinach and Sweet Red Pepper Muffins

Prep Time: 15 mins **Cook Time:** 25 mins **Total Time:** 40 mins

MAKES 12 SERVINGS

INGREDIENTS

- ❖ 2 eggs
- ❖ 2 ¾ cups all-purpose flour
- ❖ ¼ cup sugar
- ❖ 1 teaspoon paprika
- ❖ 2 teaspoons baking powder
- ❖ ¾ cup low-fat milk
- ❖ ½ cup extra virgin olive oil
- ❖ ¾ cup feta, crumbled

- ❖ 1/3 cup jarred Florina peppers, drained and patted dry
- ❖ ¾ teaspoon salt
- ❖ 1 ¼ cup spinach, thinly sliced

INSTRUCTIONS

1. Preheat the oven to 375F. Mix sugar, flour, baking powder, paprika, and salt in a bowl. Mix eggs, olive oil, and milk in another bowl.
2. Add wet ingredients to dry and mix until blended. Add spinach, fetaand peppers and mix well.
3. Line a muffin pan with liners and add the mixture to them equally. Bake for 25 minutes. Let cool for 10 minutes. Remove from the tray. Cool for 2 hours and serve.

Peanut Butter Banana Greek Yogurt Bowl

Prep Time: 15 mins **Cook Time:** 0 mins **Total Time:** 15 mins

MAKES 4 SERVINGS

INGREDIENTS

- ❖ 2 medium bananas, sliced
- ❖ 4 cups vanilla Greek yogurt
- ❖ ¼ cup peanut butter 1 teaspoon nutmeg
- ❖ ¼ cup flax seed meal

INSTRUCTIONS

1. Divide the yogurt equally among 4 bowls and add banana slices to it. Add peanut butter to a bowl and microwave for 40 seconds.

2. Add 1 tablespoon peanut butter over each bowl. Add nutmeg and flaxseed meal to each bowl. Serve.

Butter Walnut and Raisin Cookies

Prep Time: 15 mins **Cook Time:** 15 mins **Total Time:** 15 mins

MAKES 8 SERVINGS

INGREDIENTS

- ❖ ½ teaspoon pure almond extract
- ❖ ½ teaspoon pure vanilla extract
- ❖ 2 tablespoons rum
- ❖ ½ cup almond flour
- ❖ 1 stick butter, room temperature
- ❖ 1/3 cup cornflour
- ❖ 2 tablespoons Truvia
- ❖ ¼ cup raisins
- ❖ 1/3 cup walnuts, ground

INSTRUCTIONS

1. In a small bowl, place rum and raisins and allow to sit for 15-minutes. In a mixing dish, beat the butter with Truvia, vanilla, and almond extract until light and fluffy. Then, throw in both types of flour and ground almonds.

2. Fold in the soaked raisins.

3. Continue mixing until it forms a dough. Cover and store in the fridge for about 20-minutes. Meanwhile, preheat the air-fryer to 330°Fahrenheit. Roll the dough into small cookies and place them in an air-fryer cake pan; gently press each cookie with a spoon. Bake cookies for 15-minutes.

CPSIA information can be obtained
at www.ICGtesting.com
Printed in the USA
BVHW012329150321
602550BV00005B/612